Crusades

The Hidden History of the Crusaders and the Conspiracies that Followed

Conrad Bauer

ISBN: 978-1983687662

Printed in the United States

MAPLEWOOD
PUBLISHING

Contents

A Brief Program Note—Should we Politicize the Crusades? 1

Marching Toward Holy Ground _____3

The People's Crusade and Other Misadventures _____9

The Real Crusade Begins_____15

Holy Land in Crusading Hands _____21

The "Kingdom of Heaven" is at Hand_____27

The Second Crusade _____33

The Third Crusade and the Leper King_____37

The Great Miracle _____41

Conspiratorial Intrigue at Constantinople _____47

The Last Days of the Crusades _____53

The Hidden Christian Kingdom _____59

From Prester John to Genghis Khan _'_____63

The Final Crusaders and The Dangers Within _____67

The Ottoman Empire and the Canceled Crusade _____73

The Lesser Crusades and the Sick Man of Europe _____79

The Conspiracy of Silence_____85

Also by Conrad Bauer _____87

Appendix A: Further Reading and References _____91

Image Credits _____93

A Brief Program Note—Should we Politicize the Crusades?

The series of historical events known as the *Crusades*, although originating over 1000 years ago, have been invoked with increasing frequency in recent decades, and there is a tendency for the West to be apologetic about the conflict. But unlike the myth many people have come to believe, the Crusades were not an example of Dark Age, bloodthirsty European bandits spontaneously attempting to invade and colonize the Middle East.

The reason Pope Urban II launched the first Crusade (in the year 1099), was not to initiate a conflict, but rather as a rescue mission to render aid to the Christians who were being persecuted by conquering Muslim armies. The Crusaders weren't the aggressors, they were the defenders. There was violence, certainly. But the Crusades would never have

1

happened if it wasn't for the Muslim persecution of Christians that prompted it in the first place.

You see, as much as some would like to politicize the Crusades to fit their particular world view or narrative, they sometimes forget some of the facts. And the biggest fact so often forgotten was that before the rise of Islam, almost all of North Africa and the Middle East were Christian nations. But by 700 A.D. these previously Christian realms had all fallen under the sword of Islam. Places like Egypt and Syria weren't converted by charismatic preachers, they were forcibly brought into submission to Islam by way of violence.

Fast forward about 400 years to the first Crusade of 1099, and Muslim aggressors were on the march again, vigorously attempting to conquer and subjugate the Greek Orthodox Christians of the Byzantine Empire (based out of modern-day Turkey) in Eastern Europe. It was on behalf of these besieged Christian brethren to the east that the pope issued his call to arms. He was simply doing what he believed to be his Christian and moral duty—to protect Christians who were being brutally attacked by a relentless aggressor. This was a defensive act.

Defense for their neighbors and ultimately, defense for themselves. As you can see, these events from over 1000 years ago are still rather highly charged, but here in this book we will do our best to navigate through those turbulent waters.

Marching Toward Holy Ground

The first Crusade was called on November 27th, 1095, after an official envoy was sent from the former capital of the Byzantine Empire, Constantinople (modern-day Istanbul). The Byzantines, situated partially in Eastern Europe and partially in the landmass often described as "Asia Minor," were actually the remnants of the eastern half of the Roman Empire. The Roman Empire, which had reached its maximum territorial expansion around 300 A.D., encompassed the entire Mediterranean world and had holdings throughout Europe, the Middle East, and North Africa.

Here is a map of the Roman Empire at the height of its territorial expansion.

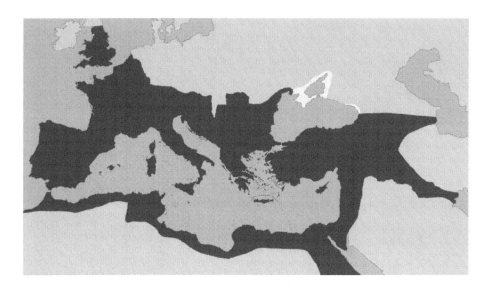

However, this massive territory would soon prove difficult to administer in its entirety so it was divided into two halves, a western half and an eastern half. It was the Emperor Constantine who would found the capital of the eastern half of the Roman Empire in 330 A.D. He built the city upon the grounds of the former Greek colony of Byzantium, and called it New Rome. But posthumously it would be named in his honor, as "Constantinople."

And so it was that about 800 years after its founding, this once great imperial capital was almost entirely surrounded by armed encampments of a relentless enemy that wanted to snuff out the ancient metropolis for good. This 1000-year-old civilization was on the brink of collapse. The Muslim Turks had at this point already infiltrated almost all of the Anatolian lands south of Constantinople, depriving the Byzantines of the vital fields that were traditionally farmed to feed its citizens.

And soon they would be at the very gates of the city. The pope then took the details of these recent events, and like a medieval news bulletin, called for a council in Clermont, France to address the dire situation that the Eastern Orthodox Christians were facing. These tidings were then followed by a clarion call to all able-bodied men of Europe to take up their arms to defend the Christian faithful who were being threatened at Muslim hands.

In this missive the pope not only extolled his audience to help make good on the Byzantine Emperor's request of aid to Constantinople, but also to recover previously Christian lands that had been lost to the Muslim advance some 400 years before—and the crown jewel of these lost lands of former Christian dominion to be recovered was that of Israel, or as it was then called, simply "The Holy Land." In order to understand how the Crusaders came to desire the recovery of what they deemed to be lost, you must first understand how it is that they lost it in the first place.

Israel, of course, did not originally belong to Christians or Muslims; it was the homeland of the Jewish people and the cradle of Judaism. Jesus, too, came from Israel, however, and so did Christianity. Christianity first came to prominence in the 1st Century A.D., when Israel was firmly locked under Roman rule. The Romans themselves at this time were polytheistic pagans, and cared neither for Judaism nor Christianity. For the first few centuries of the religion, Christianity was considered just one among many offshoots of Judaism, and was simply referred to as the "Nazarene Sect."

It was called this because Jesus carried out much of his early ministry in the Northern Israeli town of Nazareth. It wasn't until Roman Emperor Constantine issued the Edict of Milan in 313 A.D. that an official toleration of Christianity was proclaimed. Christianity would then soon move from its "tolerated" status to becoming the official religion of the entire Empire. This meant that Israel—for all intents and purposes—was now a Christian state. And the most important one—since it was the land from whence Christianity had originated in the first place.

It was Constantine who built the Church of the Holy Sepulcher in the Israeli capital of Jerusalem on the site of what was said to be Jesus's tomb. In the next few centuries several other holy sites would be ordained as well. The first disruption of this Christian dominion over Israel occurred in 614 A.D., when the King of Persia, Khosrau II, sent out a massive invasion force and successfully seized and conquered the Holy Land. However, the Persian occupation would only last a few years before the Byzantines rallied enough will and manpower to drive the Persians out.

It was a massive effort to reclaim Israel, and it came at a great cost to the Byzantines in both treasure and manpower. As a result, the exhausted Byzantine Empire was completely unprepared when a new threat rose up out of the Middle East in the name of Islam. The beleaguered Byzantines were still recovering from the war with Persia, and were unable to withstand this new onslaught, so soon on the heels of the last.

As a result, the Byzantines were forced to abandon any claim to Israel, and by the time of Pope Urban II's first call for a Crusade in 1095, Israel had already been under Muslim control for about 400 years. For most of us today, after an elapse of four centuries, it would probably seem like a foregone conclusion that the current occupiers were there to stay. After all, a country like the United States is only around 250 years old, yet most in North America would not expect U.S. citizens to be suddenly ousted by the previous residents (the Native Americans) any time soon.

But for the Crusaders, who viewed the Holy Land as the eternal home of their faith, 400 years was not enough time to deter their march toward its reclamation. Even though the most imminent threat to Christianity was lurking at the gates of Constantinople, the real prize that appealed to the crusading Christian heart was the reclamation of what they believed to be hallowed and sacred ground—their eternal Holy Land.

The People's Crusade and Other Misadventures

The launch of the first official Crusade was tentatively set for August 15th, 1096. The pope, a man of great pragmatism, wanted to make sure there was enough time to make proper provision for the crusaders, and relied upon the nobility of Europe to maintain order in the ranks. Pope Urban desired a crack group of serious soldiers, and wished for them to maintain the utmost discipline during their pilgrimage. He wished to avoid some of the more scandalous abuses that would later come to plague some of the so-called "Christian" warriors who were a little more difficult to control.

But the pope's insistence on order didn't stop other, less seasoned religious leaders from trying to take the initiative from him. And the most famous among these was a countryside preacher known as Peter the Hermit. Taking on a visage resembling John the Baptist, dressed in ragged clothes and preaching in the wilderness, this firebrand orator set and stoked the fires of Christian passion. Peter the Hermit was said to have traveled from town to town on a donkey, spreading the news that the Holy Land needed Christian defenders.

Although the official crusade was still several weeks away, this overachieving evangelist with his impassioned rhetoric was able to convince the everyday people of the villages to drop everything they were doing and follow him. These eager beaver crusaders didn't want to wait for the organized group of professional fighters led by Europe's leading barons and knights; they were ready to go it alone. Blinded by religious zeal, they followed Peter mostly on foot, equipped with only a song and a prayer. All of them firmly trusted that God would lead them to victory over his enemies.

They looked toward the biblical scriptures—especially the Old Testament accounts of when the Hebrews first claimed the "promised land" of Israel—as their blueprints for success. These mostly uneducated but deeply devout Christians seemed to truly believe that if the God of the Old Testament led the ancient Hebrews to the promised land, he would lead them as well.

Peter the Hermit stirred up the hearts of thousands, and unlike the pope, who relegated the main crusade to mostly knights, nobles, and trained fighters, Peter didn't put any limits on the divine mission he was proclaiming. He called for everyone to take up their cross against the enemies of God. Later known as the "People's Crusade," this unofficial call to arms brought thousands of men, women, and children from all social classes, rich and poor alike, together to march on the Holy Land. In some cases, whole families flocked to the People's Crusade, ready to fight their opponents with nothing more than brooms, clubs, frying pans, and other items that would barely qualify as weapons.

This group began their march in April of 1096. They arrived in Constantinople later that summer. One can only imagine the look on the Byzantine Emperor's face when this bedraggled and filthy lot showed up at his doorstep. This ragtag crew of amateurs was not exactly what he'd expected when he asked the powerful armies of Western Europe for their aid. Nevertheless, he received Peter the Hermit and his People's Crusade with open arms and allowed them to create encampments around Constantinople until they could figure out their next move. But this group had already traveled many miles, and most of them were on the brink of starvation.

Left destitute in the squalor of their encampments on the outskirts of Constantinople, the people began to create a great disturbance through massive foraging campaigns for food and even outright theft from the farms of Byzantine citizens. In order to meet the needs of his "visitors," the Byzantine emperor had to move very quickly to supply the hungry Westerners with food rations in order to prevent a riot from breaking out. Having just about all he could stomach of these early crusaders, the emperor then quickly agreed to dispatch them onto his enemies, and on August 6th, set them loose in the Anatolian plains south of Constantinople to embark upon their first engagement with the armies of Islam.

At first, the group contented themselves to make sporadic raids, the first of which was against the Muslim-held city of Nicaea. This was actually the place where Roman Emperor Constantine had convened the Council of Nicaea, which crafted the Nicene Creed for Christianity in 325 A.D. Despite its historic significance, Peter the Hermit's People's Crusade now only saw it as a gathering of infidels, and ruthlessly pillaged the town. Despite their lack of proper armor and weapons, by a mixture of sheer brute force and simply catching the townspeople by surprise, this first encounter left these unlikely warriors feeling fairly victorious.

But in their second engagement they would not be so lucky. Militias of Turkish Muslims, made aware of the threat that had crossed into their borders, intercepted the ragtag band of Christian fighters and managed to capture the entire group. It is said that these captured men, women, and children were then forced to convert to Islam, or face immediate execution. Those who refused were indeed executed, and those who renounced Christ as their savior and pledged their allegiance to Mohammed were packed up in caravans and shipped off to begin new lives as slaves, never to be heard from by their family members back home, ever again.

Interestingly, while this was happening to his followers, the pied piper who had started it all and convinced these common, everyday people to follow him, Peter the Hermit, was safely ensconced in the Emperor's royal palace in Constantinople. It is said that of all the people he led to fight in the People's Crusade, Peter himself was the only person to have made it out alive.

The sheer improbability of the Peter the Hermit and the People's Crusade has led to quite a few conspiracy theories. One of the most prominent was that Peter was an agent of the Pope with an insidious ulterior motive. According to these theorists, Peter and his handlers knew full well that his followers would be decimated, but wished to send them anyway. At the time, Europe was facing a massive population boom, especially among the poor, leading to widespread unrest and unemployment as landless peasants aimlessly wandered the countryside.

Those who promote this conspiracy theory believe that Peter the Hermit was purposely contracted to lead these troublesome people right out of Europe. There is, of course, no real evidence that this was anyone's intention. The most likely explanation for the fervor of the People's Crusade was simply the religious enthusiasm that the pope had stirred up. These fires were then stoked and carried on by a well-meaning but grossly unprepared and ill-informed preacher, Peter the Hermit.

In reality, it seems to have been a particularly potent mixture of pure religious zeal and blissful ignorance that led to the misadventure of the People's Crusade. And this was most likely exactly the sort of the thing the pope was trying to avoid in the first place, when he stressed the need for order and discipline in the ranks.

Pope Urban had specifically ordered his bishops not to take any vows to fight. Conspiracy theories aside, from what we can gather, having a throng of poor village people aimlessly wandering into faraway battlefields would be counterproductive to Pope Urban II's aims. He only wanted the most able-bodied and professional soldiery to take up the call, in order to minimize misadventure and maximize the Crusade.

The Real Crusade Begins

The first official Crusading army to arrive at the gates of Constantinople was that of Hugh of Vermandois, a prince of France. Hugh managed to arrive faster than the other official dispatches because of the direct path of travel he chose, which had his army traveling by boat over the Adriatic Sea for the last leg of their journey. His contingent was also smaller than the other crusading armies, making it much more mobile. When Hugh's group arrived, like Peter the Hermit's ragtag band, these trained soldiers were allowed to build an encampment just outside of the city.

Hugh, meanwhile, was invited into the Emperor's palace to discuss a strategy for the ensuing conflict. But what was foremost on Byzantine Emperor Alexius's mind was not how to fight the Muslim Turks, but what should happen to any lands that were confiscated from them. Emperor Alexius was deeply worried that, after liberating formerly Byzantine lands, his Christian friends from the west would keep them for themselves instead of returning them. He asked Hugh to swear an oath that any former holdings of the Byzantine Empire that were reclaimed would be returned to the Byzantines, the rightful holders of such property.

After some additional prompting, Hugh grudgingly agreed. Similar oaths would be given to the Emperor by other leading figures of the crusade, but in the end, the temptation of establishing their own crusader kingdoms would be too hard to resist. Most had forfeited any land and wealth they had back home in order to make the arduous journey to defend Christendom, and even the noblest of Christians couldn't help but feel a bit cheated if they didn't get anything in return.

So it should have come as no surprise—oath or no oath—that they would try to carve out their own piece of the pie. The first territory to fall into crusader hands was that of Nicaea, the same town that Peter the Hermit's group of ruffians had plundered before their capture. There were Turkish garrisons posted in the city, but it is said that they greatly underestimated this latest crusader invasion force. With the recent experience of crushing the poorly equipped band of Peter the Hermit's People's Crusade, the Muslim defenders no doubt believed this new group of Europeans would be just easily dispatched as well.

This was not the case however, and on May 21st, 1097 Nicaea was captured and her Turkish defenders were defeated. The Turks, reeling from this decisive victory, then turned to diplomacy, and opened up a dialogue with the Byzantines. These discussions led to an agreement in which the Byzantine Emperor promised to secure the city and protect the "life and property" of all Muslims who chose to remain. These negotiations went right over the heads of the crusaders by whom the reconquest of the city had come about.

No one told them about the deal, and the very next day, they awoke to Byzantine ships in every port, and banners being strewn from every window, wall, and parapet. In the case of Nicaea, it seemed that the Byzantines weren't going to wait around and see if the crusaders would make good on their pledge to return reconquered lands; they decided to take the initiative themselves. In the end, for their labors, all the crusaders received were a few gifts given to their commanders, and the profuse gratitude of the emperor.

But after a few banquets in their honor and several rounds of thanks, the brave men who had left it all behind to fight for Christendom were basically shooed away from the land they had just reclaimed. Unable to stay in Nicaea, the crusading armies were then forced to regroup without a base of operations, and they headed further south, toward the fortified city of Antioch. They journeyed for a few months in the desert, enduring the merciless heat and a severe lack of food and water, until on October 21st, 1097, the tremendous walls of fortified Antioch were visible on the horizon.

The crusaders then led a siege against the city that would last for nearly eight months. As they maintained this standoff, conditions for the Christian warriors were going from bad to worse. In order to survive, they were reduced to the most rudimentary foraging, eating grass, and in some cases even seeds collected from manure dropped from beasts of the field. Worst of all for the Christian knights whose whole image and prestige was connected to their trusty steed, many of these noblemen found themselves having to put the sword to their own horses just to have something they could eat.

They were unable to break down the fortified walls of Antioch and all seemed lost, but then a breakthrough came—not from without, but from within. The crusaders had been in a secret dialogue with one of the city's night watchmen, and incredibly, were able to bribe him into letting them climb over the wall and open the gate so the rest of the crusaders could just waltz right through, unopposed.

It is interesting to note that there is an ancient conspiracy theory attached to this event. Recalling this disaster, for centuries, there were Muslims who whispered the possibility that the man who allowed these foreign crusaders into the city was not a man at all, but was actually a jinn!

In the Islamic tradition jinn are not human, but are supernatural shapeshifters and tricksters somewhat akin to the mischievous sprites of Irish folklore, leprechauns, elves, and fairies. Or as others have pointed out, they also bear some resemblance to the terrifying "skin walkers" of Native American lore. According to the Islamic tradition, jinn do not take sides in human affairs, but are equal opportunity troublemakers. And if this conspiracy were to be believed, the prospect of the chaos and carnage that would be unleashed upon the sleeping city by the crusaders must have too much for this mischievous jinn to resist!

In reality, it probably wasn't too hard for the crusaders to find a sympathetic collaborator. Antioch had previously been part of the Byzantine Empire and had only fallen into Muslim hands in 1085, barely a decade prior to the time of the first crusade. The majority of Antioch's population was still Greek Christian, and any number of them may have had reason to allow the western Christian crusaders to slip through the gates. At any rate, once access was gained, the crusader army was able to pour into the city.

And by the time the Muslim Turkish authorities realized what was happening it was too late. Antioch was now a possession of the foreign crusaders they had tried so hard to keep out.

However, the crusading Christians didn't have long to rest, and soon had to fend off a massive relief force that was galloping right toward them at full speed. And to make matters worse, even though the Christian fighters were now safely ensconced inside the massive walls of Antioch, they were still starving. It was their own previous siege of the city that had ensured no provisions had been supplied for several months, and as a result, practically all the storehouses of Antioch were completely empty.

With the distress of the defenders mounting, some lost their nerve and attempted to make a run for it. Some of these deserters were then rounded up and captured by the approaching Muslim forces, who decided to make an example of them by impaling these runaways on stakes and proudly displaying their dismembered corpses right in front of the ramparts of Antioch. The larger Muslim army had now completely surrounded the city, and many of the crusaders began to consider the irony of the position they were in.

Had they spent months besieging Antioch only to become trapped inside its walls and hopelessly besieged themselves? But it was in the depths of this despair that the visions of the faithful seemed to increase, and one of the greatest conspiracies of the Crusades took shape; the conspiracy of the Spear of Destiny.

Holy Land in Crusading Hands

By the time of the Crusades, the idea of the "Holy Lance" or as it was later referred to, the "Spear of Destiny" was already widely known. The legend originates directly from the biblical account of Jesus's crucifixion, and describes Jesus being pierced in the side by a Roman soldier. In this biblical account found in the book of John, this is just one detail of the event that isn't elaborated on. But later the story expanded, and even put a spotlight on the spear-wielding soldier himself.

It wasn't until the 4th century that apocryphal, extra biblical narrative presented in the Gospel of Nicodemus expanded on this aspect of the crucifixion, with the spear-wielding soldier being referred to as Longinus. It was apparently from here that the backstory of Longinus and the so-called Spear of Destiny really took off. It was believed that whosoever possessed this spear would be a master of war and invincible in battle. And since then, this holy relic is said to have been recovered and lost several times.

So it was, in 1098 A.D., during the darkest hours of the besieged crusaders at Antioch, this legend conveniently resurfaced once again. Talk of the spear began anew when a traveling soldier and mystic named Peter Bartholomew claimed to be experiencing some fairly extraordinary visions, including a visitation of St. Andrew. This patron saint supposedly informed Peter Bartholomew that the relic of the "Holy Lance" was buried in the grounds of Antioch.

Not everyone was ready to believe Bartholomew, but after a few strange signs in the night sky, such as a massive meteor that seemed to crash land right in the middle of the Turkish encampment outside the city wall, people became more receptive. And on the morning of June 15th, after attending a service in Antioch's Cathedral of St. Peter, Bartholomew, as if in a trance, suddenly converged on one spot of the church and implored those around him to begin digging.

It is said that several hours of excavation passed but no one could find anything. But then, right when his followers were about to give up, Peter Bartholomew threw himself down into one of the dig sites and began frantically clawing at the dirt with his fingers. Seconds later he cried out in exultation to let the onlookers know he'd found something. And holding it up in the light for them to see what he found, it did indeed appear to be the old, antiquated head of a spear. Most were overjoyed at the sight and became true believers that something miraculous had occurred.

But later sceptics would suggest that perhaps Bartholomew quite literally had a few tricks up his sleeve that day, and had planted the old spear tip down in the hole himself. But really, in the end, the voracity of the item (or where it came from), didn't matter all that much. As long as the people believed it, the reaction was the same, and the morale of the crusaders went through the roof. Amazingly, they no longer despaired of their condition, and were filled with the utmost confidence that they would go on to victory. And history records that—against all odds—they would be right in that assumption.

The crusaders poured out of the confines of Antioch on June 28th, and fought with such unmitigated ferocity and fervor that the Turkish militia that had been arrayed against them was quickly beaten back. Their opponents couldn't quite explain this incredible reversal of fate, but for the crusaders it was because God was on their side and the Spear of Destiny was in their hands. And they hoped that their divine providence would next lead them on to their ultimate goal: the reclamation of the Holy Land's capital city of Jerusalem.

They arrived at the gates of Jerusalem in 1099 A.D. From outside the city, the crusaders stared in fascination upon the domed churches and mosques that dotted the landscape for miles. They were ready to traverse the streets of this most holy of cities, but the massive stone walls of Jerusalem prevented their entrance. Unsure of what else to do, it is said that the leaders of the crusade took a detour to the nearby Mount of Olives.

They did so both to experience this biblical locale, as well as to confer about what their next move might be. It is also here at the Mount of Olives that the history of the Crusades takes another sharp turn into the world of conspiracy. It has long been stated that the leaders of the crusaders met a very strange character who lived on this mountain. They took this man to be a prophet and holy man, and were apparently quite impressed with him. It is said that the man encouraged their march on Jerusalem, telling them, "If you attack the city tomorrow on the 9th hour, the Lord will deliver it into your hands."

And when some of those among them protested at these grandiose statements, informing the mystic that they needed to build siege engines to break through Jerusalem's defenses, the monk dismissed such things as immaterial, telling them "these things do not matter." All that really matters, he said is "faith— faith in God, faith in His promises, and faith in His miraculous power." The majority of the crusaders took the monk at his word, and as he instructed, the next day they launched an assault on Jerusalem's outer wall. Incredibly, without even a ladder, crusaders climbed up the walls with their bare hands!

The Muslim defenders were shocked to see the strange foreigner's determination, but after they breached the outer wall, they found the inner wall to be too much for them. These walls were 50 feet high, and there was no way they could be breached or climbed without proper siege equipment. But they were in luck, because not too long after this scene played out, scout ships from England and Genoa were spotted in the port of neighboring Jaffa. The crusaders were able to take much-needed supplies from the ships and use them to begin building the siege engines they would need to take the inner court of Jerusalem.

With the help of a couple of engineers from Genoa, the crusaders managed to build a giant battering ram, catapults, and towering siege engines that could be used to breach Jerusalem's walls. They began their assault on July 13th, 1099, with a force of about 15,000 men. Near the old portal known as "Herod's Gate," they took a battering ram and used it to decimate a large chunk of the wall near the gate. The Christian knights then charged through. The defenders were ready, however, and unleashed a multitude of arrows from their bows as the crusaders stepped through the gap.

As these fighters gained access to the lower reaches of the courtyard, siege engines were being placed right up at the ramparts. Jerusalem's defenders frantically did their best to fight off these mechanized beasts of wood, completely obliterating one of them with "Greek fire." (Greek fire was a secret weapon that the Muslims had learned about from the Byzantines, a gelatinous, highly flammable substance that could be thrown onto targets, sticking to them. Flaming arrows were then shot at the target and upon making contact with the napalm-like gel, would burst into flames that were very difficult to put out.)

Several crusaders were killed or badly maimed during their efforts, but eventually one of the siege engines was able to get close enough to lower a ladder down onto Jerusalem's walls, granting the crusaders access to the city. After another round of quick but fierce fighting inside the city walls, the Muslim defenders fled to the famed Al-Aqsa mosque to hole themselves up for one final stand against the crusaders.

But this last stand never occurred. After a few rounds of negotiations, the peace of Jerusalem was bought by the crusaders not by force of arms, but by a handsome payout to the last resistors. The last defenders of Jerusalem took their payment and fled, and with this last retreating remnant of Muslim rule, Jerusalem was a Christian city. For the first time in 400 years, the Holy Land was firmly in Christian hands.

The "Kingdom of Heaven" is at Hand

Ever since Christ himself walked through the streets of Jerusalem 2000 years ago and proclaimed, "The Kingdom of Heaven is at hand!" Christians have argued over what exactly this "Kingdom of Heaven" was meant to be. Most Christians today believe that the kingdom Jesus referred to was not a physical kingdom on Earth, but rather, a reference to Heaven itself.

But for the crusaders who had just carved out their own very real kingdom in the Holy Land, the Kingdom of Heaven truly was at hand. Officially named the "Kingdom of Jerusalem," this first crusader state was founded in the year 1099. The crown of this kingdom was given to a French knight named Godfrey de Bouillon. Although Godfrey refused to be called *king*, stating that only "Christ is king," he did take on the title of "Protector of the Holy Sepulcher." This wasn't exactly an easy task.

Even as other crusaders began to leave, Godfrey and his reduced number of soldiers were expected to protect and administer wide swaths of land inhabited by people who were mostly alien to them. Although in foreign territory, these European knights sought to bring a little bit of home-styled rule to the Middle East, in what researchers of this time period would later call a transplant of Europe's "vassals and castles" directly onto Middle Eastern soil.

The Kingdom of Jerusalem would eventually encompass the entire state of Israel as well as Lebanon, and even small sections of Egypt and Syria. The man leading this kingdom, Godfrey, was a knight of the highest order, highly respected, and cut from the same cloth that would later produce the order of the Knights Templar. Even so, fate would not allow Godfrey to rule over the Kingdom of Jerusalem for very long, and just one year after he proclaimed himself to be its protector, on July 18th, 1100, he abruptly passed away.

Incidentally, there is a bit of conspiracy surrounding his death. According to some reports, Godfrey had been out on an expedition near the town of Caesarea, when the Muslim ruler of that city, feigning goodwill, requested his audience. Godfrey had a formidable host with him, and not perceiving any threat from this petty emir, decided to grant his request. The emir was very friendly and cordial, discussing the latest happenings in the land, and by all accounts they had a good discussion.

At one point during the gathering one of the emir's servants brought out a plate of fruit from which the emir offered Godfrey an apple. Then, in a scene straight out of *Snow White*, or perhaps even the garden of Eden, Godfrey took a bite out of the apple. The emir, seeing that Godfrey bit the apple (so the legend goes) then claimed he had some urgent matters he had to attend to and quickly bid his guests farewell. According to this conspiracy theory, no sooner than Godfrey and his men mounted their horses and began to leave Caesarea, the crusading leader fell terribly ill.

His body was instantly racked with episodes of violent vomiting, and it is said that only with an immense struggle did they manage to reach the nearby crusader stronghold of Jaffa. Here he was immediately confined to bed and those in the town with medical knowledge tried their best to save him, but it was too late. The poison had taken its hold and Godfrey passed away on July 18th, despite their best efforts.

This is only one theory that has been presented to explain Godfrey's sudden illness, and has never been proven. At any rate, it can't be denied that it was extremely odd for this perfectly healthy, robust crusading knight to deteriorate so rapidly.

It would be Godfrey's brother Baldwin who would then be crowned on December 25th, 1100, in great ceremony, as the first "official king" of the kingdom of Jerusalem. Baldwin had apparently no qualms with the title and accepted the reality that in order for the kingdom to survive, it needed a strong leader—it needed a king. It was under Baldwin that the order of knights known as the "Hospitallers" was created.

Working as a kind of ancient medic force, these men came to specialize in field medicine and treatment for trauma. It could even be argued that perhaps it was the sudden and quick demise of Godfrey that inspired the citizens of Jerusalem to invest in medical treatment. It was the Hospitallers who created entire houses to care for the sick, which became known as "hospitals," a tremendous innovation at the time. There was nothing quite like it before.

Baldwin worked hard to consolidate his kingdom, expanding its territory in all directions. And by the time of his passing on April 2nd, 1118, nearly the entire coast of Israel proper would be under the kingdom's dominion. The death of Baldwin, the first king of Jerusalem, left a succession crisis in its wake. Baldwin did not have any children to pass his throne to, so just prior to his demise he had requested that his brother, Eustace, succeed him as his heir.

But the barons who handled the transition felt differently about it, and chose another Baldwin—Baldwin of Bourcq—to take the throne as Baldwin II. Baldwin was a decisive leader, but met several setbacks in his reign—culminating with his capture by enemy forces in April 1123. Baldwin II's freedom was eventually purchased for a large ransom and he returned to his throne in Jerusalem. Baldwin II would spend the rest of his life perfecting monastic orders of knights, and in particular, the Knights Templar.

It was Baldwin II who oversaw the conversion of the Al-Aqsa mosque into the Temple of Solomon. It is from this temple that the name for the Templar order is derived.

The order of the Knights Templar would receive official acceptance by the pope in 1128. With the acceptance of the order came certain rules. First of all, the knights were to engage in regular prayer, literally designated to be "prayer warriors." There were some other minor stipulations such as abstaining from the consumption of meat four days a week, and avoiding any gambling or games of chance. But besides prayer, occasionally fasting from meat, and staying away from the poker table, the main vow that the Templar Knights had to take and adhere to was a pledge to protect Christian shrines and their pilgrims. More important than anything else, was the honoring of this holy mission.

In the Knights' official charter it was stated that they were not to retreat unless they are being attacked by more than three opponents at once. This meant that even if one solitary knight escorting a group of Christian pilgrims or guarding a shrine, was beset upon by three attackers, he would have no choice but to stand his ground.

The designated leader of the Templars was called a Grand Master, a term that Freemasons would later use to connote the leader of their lodge. The first Grand Master of the Templars was a man named Hugh de Payens, a crusader veteran who hailed from the village of Payens in France. The Grand Master of Jerusalem soon became quite an authority figure and ultimately was only answerable to the pope in Italy and Baldwin II, the king of Jerusalem. The sovereign, Baldwin II, died on August 21st, 1131. Since Baldwin II had no sons, it was incumbent upon his daughter Melisandre to gain the throne as the queen of the Kingdom of Jerusalem.

In 1143, Queen Melisandre then gave the throne to her son Baldwin III, staying in the background as a co-ruler. It was around this time that the second crusade was launched.

The Second Crusade

The call for a second Crusade began when the crusader state of Edessa fell to Muslim forces in 1144. The Christians were very much on the defensive at this point, and were hoping that a second call to arms in Western Europe would bring them the aid they needed. Initiated by Pope Eugene III, what would become known as the Second Crusade was launched in 1147.

Much of the fervor of this crusade didn't come from Pope Eugene III, but rather a popular Cistercian monk—Bernard de Clairvaux. This charismatic firebrand delivered sermons to large audiences extolling the virtues of taking part in a renewed Holy War. He preached for others to take up the cross and travel to the Middle East, and even went so far as to have several piles of cloth cross patches on hand, so that as thousands of persuaded parishioners came forward to "take up the cross" for the crusade he preached about, they would have a cross literally sown onto their tunic to remind them of the commitment they had made.

The Second Crusade was led by armies from both France and Germany. Due to the intense rivalry between the two nations, many have noted that it might have been more successful if it were just France or just Germany alone that took up the call. At any rate, the two nations were not united in their effort, and the endeavor was fraught with bitter disagreement from the beginning. As a result, this crusade would not see the same success as its predecessor. In battle after battle, the crusaders would come up short, and in the end the Second Crusade has to be considered almost a complete failure.

Since this second wave of crusaders did nothing but embolden and encourage the armies of Islam with their easy victories over them, many feel that the Second Crusade actually made things worse for the Kingdom of Jerusalem, rather than better. And as the last remnants fled back to Europe in tatters, it seemed increasingly clear to the new generation (who had been born and raised in the Kingdom of Jerusalem) that if they were to be saved, they would have to save themselves.

Meanwhile Baldwin III, king of Jerusalem, had become a ruler in his own right. Without any help from European outsiders, on August 19th, 1153, Baldwin III successfully captured the final Muslim holdout on the Israeli coast, and seized the fortified city of Ascalon to incorporate into his kingdom. Ascalon, situated just north of Egypt's Sinai desert, had long been a troublesome thorn in the side of the Kingdom of Jerusalem. It was from here that Egyptian Muslims launched raids and other attacks against the crusader states, and shutting it down had been a priority from the beginning.

With this military victory under his belt, Baldwin III then sought an additional political win by forming an alliance with the Byzantine Empire in 1158, and even marrying the Byzantine emperor's niece Theodora, hoping to make an even more permanent partnership with their Orthodox Christian neighbors through family ties. But if those around him were hoping that this union would provide an heir to the kingdom with Byzantine blood, they were disappointed.

Baldwin III passed away just a few years after his marriage, in February of 1163, with no heir apparent. Closing the chapter on what could have been a great union of Byzantine and crusader power, his successor by default was his younger brother Amalric. The next few years would be of slow decline, and many would find themselves often wondering aloud over the proclamation made a thousand years before—was the Kingdom of Heaven really at hand?

The Third Crusade and the Leper King

Almeric, the Crusader King of Jerusalem—as was all too often the case in his family—died of sudden illness on July 11th, 1774. This left the throne in the hands of his 13-year-old son, Baldwin IV. Baldwin's IV's reign seemed to be doomed from the very start. Not only was he awfully young to have the full course of statecraft thrust upon him, he was also just not physically healthy enough to lead. Although said to be extremely intelligent, he had been plagued with bouts of sickness since birth, and would eventually be diagnosed with leprosy.

It is said that the startling symptoms of this disease were first noticed when Baldwin IV was just a small child. He was playing with some other children under the eyes of one of his guardians when his chaperone noticed that Baldwin seemed oddly immune to pain. The kids were wrestling with each other, and playing rough, as kids often do. As they were in the midst of their games, Baldwin's personal attendant grew increasingly alarmed to see cuts, scrapes, and bruises appearing on the young man's arms and legs, yet Baldwin IV seemed happily oblivious to his injuries.

It now became apparent to his royal retainers that something was very wrong. Baldwin was examined by his personal physician shortly after this, and it was discovered that the youth's numbness to pain was a result of the early stages of leprosy. This was obviously an unsettling realization, and by the time Baldwin IV was crowned king, rumors of his illness were already widespread. It was just another reason for the citizens of the Kingdom of Jerusalem to feel uneasy during the early days of Baldwin IV's reign.

Besides the rumors swirling around the state of the King's health, there was growing fear over the very real military threats that were building around the kingdom's borders. And the main threat that had surfaced was a charismatic and powerful new Muslim leader by the name of Saladin. His full name in Arabic was "Al-Malik Al Nasir *Salah Al-din* Yusuf." But historians, for obvious reason, typically default to the abbreviated form of this name, Saladin, and for the purpose of this book, we will as well.

At the time of Baldwin IV's coronation, Saladin had just signed a peace treaty with the regent of Tripoli (not to be confused with the Libyan capital, this Tripoli was situated in Israel.) But this peace treaty proved to be disastrous for the Kingdom of Jerusalem since it allowed Saladin to build up strength in neighboring Syria. And as a result, Saladin was soon able to consolidate the previously scattered Muslim groups just east of the Kingdom of Jerusalem into one formidable fighting force.

Baldwin IV, as young and inexperienced as he was, understood the grave threat to his Kingdom. And so, feeling he could wait no longer, in 1176, at the age of just 15, he ordered a preemptive strike against Saladin, attacking his holdings in neighboring Damascus. This put Saladin's forces on the defensive, but Saladin soon rebounded and sent a group of 26,000 soldiers to assault the Kingdom of Jerusalem. The city itself was soon surrounded, and morale was very low.

To make matters worse, the young King's condition had deteriorated to such an extent that he was left relegated almost entirely to his bedchambers. But despite his fading health and the protests of his physicians, Baldwin IV forced himself up out of what—by all accounts—should have been his deathbed. Gathering the final strength of a dying man, Baldwin had his aides wrap his decaying flesh in bandages, and carefully place his armor and sword on his leprosy-ravaged frame.

Barely able to stand, yet somehow pushing himself forward, the Leper King was determined to fight for his people one last time. Leaving the safety of Jerusalem's walls behind, Baldwin IV led a group of just 3000 regular soldiers and a little over 60 knights to intercept Saladin's much larger army. The Muslims who encountered this Leper King were indeed quite shocked to see the leader of the crusaders covered from head to toe in bandages like a mummy. It is said that right before engaging Saladin's men, Baldwin IV got off of his horse, and from his cloak pulled out a holy relic: the "true cross."

This relic in particular seems to be another focal point of conspiracy among the crusaders, with many accounts of the Knights Templar smuggling the holy artifact out of Jerusalem during the Kingdom's last days. But in 1176 the relic is alleged to have been firmly in Baldwin IV's hands. Baldwin is said to have bowed down before the true cross and begged God for victory.

He then got back on his horse and led his men to one last charge against Saladin. To any outside observer, this small troop of crusaders should have been crushed easily by the larger, better-equipped army of Saladin.

But whether it was the miraculous power of the relic at work or not—history records a spectacular victory—and beyond all odds, the crusaders seemed to overwhelm and overcome the Muslim warriors by sheer force of will. They refused to be defeated, and fought with such ferocity that Saladin and his men had no choice but to turn around and retreat. In the end, a large portion of his army was decimated and Saladin himself almost didn't make it out of the battle alive.

After the battle, participants on both sides claimed to have witnessed strange paranormal activity centered around Baldwin IV. The Leper King appeared to take on an unearthly glow as he rode through the battlefield, slaying opponent after opponent with cold, quiet determination. The true cross he carried on his person seemed to give off an especially ghostly illumination during the course of the conflict.

Christian fighters made some even more specific claims, stating that they saw none other than the patron saint of the warrior, Saint George, watching over them, and following Baldwin IV's lead as he decimated the enemy. But the victory the Leper King delivered to his people on that day would be fleeting, and just a couple of years after their astonishing triumph, Baldwin IV would finally succumb to the leprosy that had afflicted him for so long, and his successors would soon feel the need for yet another crusade.

The Great Miracle

Soon after Baldwin IV's death in 1185, the seeds of the Kingdom of Jerusalem's demise would be planted. The great Muslim military leader Saladin had managed to unite much of the Muslim world against the crusaders and was on the march with a massive army. After luring the main fighting force of Jerusalem out into the open desert, Saladin was able to encircle the group and almost completely annihilate them. In so doing, not only was the main defense of the Kingdom felled with one blow—to the horror and shame of the few who did manage to survive—Saladin gained possession of the holy relic of the true cross.

The same item of divine power that Baldwin IV had used to lead them to victory was now being held by their arch nemesis Saladin, who mockingly held the cross upside down before him as he massacred Christians. The psychological defeat engendered by this sight was almost more unbearable than the physical death toll the crusader army had suffered. And Saladin, being the military genius that he was, probably knew exactly what he was doing to his enemies' psyches with his sacrilegious display of the cross. The combination of serious lack of manpower to defend Jerusalem, together with this psychological warfare, was working well against them.

Jerusalem was soon completely surrounded, and Saladin entered the city without a struggle on October 2nd, 1187. Several other crusader cities would follow, and in just a couple of years, the crusader kingdom that once spanned the entire breadth of Israel would be reduced to just three holdout realms in Tripoli, Antioch, and Tyre. The crusaders were now backed into a corner, hanging on to the Middle East by just a thread, and were in desperate need of major reinforcement if they were to remain even in this limited bit of real estate.

As a consequence, it was determined that a Third Crusade must be called. It is said that Pope Urban III actually died of grief when he received word that Jerusalem was captured, passing away on October 20th, 1187. But his successor, Pope Gregory VIII, did not waste any time. He only took few days to call for Europe's third Crusade to reclaim the Holy Lands that had fallen into Muslim hands.

Before this latest call to arms, the leaders of Europe had been far too busy attacking each other in their own backyards to be of much use rendering aid to faraway lands. But in Gregory's powerfully crafted address to the European heads of state he managed to convince them of the gravity of the situation. And just like Pope Urban II's impassioned pleas of nearly 100 years before, he was able to stir their hearts to action. Pope Gregory called for the kingdoms of Europe to temporarily forget their squabbles and enter into a seven-year truce, so they could combine their strength in an effort to retake the Holy Land. In this call for European reconciliation, the most bitter rivals who needed to be brought to the table were King Henry II of England, and King Philip II of France, who were embroiled in an intense conflict.

But after the Pope himself intervened in peace talks between them, the two major players of the Third Crusade, England and France, signed an official ceasefire on January 21st, 1188. They were then joined in April of 1189 by the German forces of Emperor Frederick Barbarossa. Frederick Barbarossa was the leader of the conglomerate of central European states, which at that time were called the "Holy Roman Empire."

Barbarossa was in his 70s at the time and was actually a veteran of the Second Crusade, making him the most experienced leader of this current group of crusaders. But all of his accumulated knowledge and experience was lost when he drowned in a river as his army crossed through Armenia in 1190. It was a rather undignified end to Barbarossa's highly decorated career, and it left the German host in complete disarray. Most of the German soldiers decided to disband and went home, with only a small fraction of the original fighting force continuing the journey to the Middle East.

England had faced a similar crisis when King Henry II passed away of natural causes in 1189, but the problem was quickly mitigated when his popular son, Richard the Lionheart, took over the command of Britain's army.

The combined English and French army decided to travel over sea rather than by land. They recruited Venetian ships for the task, and sailing straight across the Mediterranean, set up camp just outside of the port city of Acre in 1191.

This landing force is said to have comprised 600,000 men, and they immediately converged on the city to retake it from the Muslim occupiers. Overwhelmed and overpowered, the defenders of Acre surrendered the city to the crusaders on July 12th of that year. The king of France wouldn't stick around much longer, however, and after expressing some misgivings about the operation, he returned to France. Richard the Lionheart was now the sole authority in charge of all the crusader forces that had chosen to remain.

The next marching orders that Richard delivered to his followers was to head south down the coastline to Jaffa, since it was the closest port city to Jerusalem. Richard figured if he could secure Jaffa then he would have a more direct supply line and base of operations with which to invade Jerusalem.

Saladin, meanwhile, followed their every move. Richard had his army hug the coastline as they took as direct a route as possible to Jaffa. Not wanting to risk any major losses until the main fight was at hand, Richard ordered his men to not be lured out into open conflict.

Saladin's archers lurking in the shadows tried their best to do so, however, firing off so many arrows at times that some of the knights looked more like walking pincushions than human beings. But even with arrows sticking out of the backs of their armor, the knights dutifully followed Richard's command, and amazingly, even in the face of incredible harassment, they kept their heads down and stayed focused on their destination.

Saladin's strategy was to make the crusaders lose their patience and drag them into open warfare in the desert, just as he had done in Jerusalem several years before. But as he was rebuffed and ignored, it was Saladin who lost his patience, not the crusaders. Desperate to engage the migrating warriors, on September 7th he made the first move and struck out at them in an all-out assault. This proved to be a terrible mistake for the Muslim leader, and almost all of his army was destroyed by the crusaders.

Richard the Lionheart, meanwhile, lost hardly any men at all. It was a victory for the Christian warriors, and now even before reaching the gates of Jaffa, a victorious conclusion seemed all but imminent there as well. It was a sentiment not lost on Saladin, and sensing defeat, he withdrew all of his protection from the city, removed his fortifications, and fled to nearby Ascalon to wait out the crusader takeover. The crusaders then seized Jaffa unopposed.

After securing Jaffa, Richard then marched his men further inland and began the trek to Jerusalem. But finding that they were outmatched and that their supply lines wouldn't be able to hold out, the group made a strategic retreat back to Jaffa. Realizing that taking and holding Jerusalem was just not feasible at that time, Richard then turned away from tactics of war, toward diplomacy. He outlined a truce with Saladin that would allow the Christians to keep the land they had re-conquered along the coastline, and although Jerusalem would remain in Muslim hands, he requested that Christians be allowed safe passage as pilgrims to the Holy City.

Saladin, who was known as a very generous deal maker, agreed to all of these stipulations without hesitation. These two powerful men who were on the verge of waging one of the most climactic battles in all of history, rather than being enemies, miraculously ended up being somewhere closer to friends near the end. The Christian crusader and Muslim leader were indeed on quite good terms with each other. In a time of never-ending conflict and strife, this was one of the greatest miracles the Holy Land had ever bestowed.

Conspiratorial Intrigue at Constantinople

The Fourth Crusade was called by Pope Innocent III in the year 1202. Innocent III had just ascended to the papacy in 1198, and he had run on a platform of reclaiming the Holy Land at any cost. Pope Innocent believed that in order for Jerusalem to be reclaimed, Christians needed to form a united front—both militarily and spiritually. They were indeed rich in spirit and military might, but the one thing they lacked was money. This deficiency in finances would prove disastrous when the group arrived at the ports of Venice without enough money to pay for their voyage across the Mediterranean to the Holy Land.

The Venetians were even more frustrated about this than the crusaders, since they not only had to deal with an unpaid bill, but also the presence of a large and restless army outstaying its welcome right in their backyard. The situation was simply untenable for both parties, and something had to be done. It was then that the Venetian council came up with a plan.

As it turns out, one of the Venetian kingdom's city states, a town called Zara on the Dalmatian coast, had recently seceded from them. The Venetians desperately wanted Zara back, and since they suddenly had all these able-bodied fighters in their backyard, a plan was concocted to use the crusaders' fighting ability to their own ends as payment. The Crusaders would have their debt indefinitely suspended if they would help the Venetians get Zara back.

The crusaders were at first hesitant to accept this proposal, since the residents of Zara were Christian and they just didn't feel right about killing brethren of their own faith. But, they concluded, Venice was justified to want its territory back, and at any rate, if they refused to help, their passage across the Mediterranean would be denied and this crusade would be over before it had even begun. They felt they had no choice but to accept the offer. So, with heavy hearts they obediently shipped out with the Venetians to Zara, arriving on November 10th. At first it appeared that they wouldn't have to kill any Christians after all; the citizens of Zara apparently realized that they were hopelessly outmatched, and were ready to surrender.

But just as the Zarans were ready to sign away their rights to the Venetians, a French nobleman named Simon de Montifort intervened. Apparently disgusted with the Venetians using the crusaders as mercenaries for their own means, he went over to the Zarans and explained to them that by papal orders, the crusaders could not rightfully attack them. The, Zarans taking his word for it, then reversed course and retracted their surrender. The crusaders could not back down, and felt forced to go ahead with the attack.

The Zarans, continuing to believe that crusaders wouldn't attack fellow Christians, draped large banners over their city walls with crosses on them, but this would not be enough to deter the crusaders from fulfilling the bargain they had made with the Venetians. In a matter of days, the city of Zara fell to the crusader sword. The crusaders were now facing excommunication from the Catholic Church, which for someone of the deep faith of that era, would have felt like a fate worse than death.

The crusaders immediately dispatched messengers to Rome to plead with the pope for forgiveness. Fortunately for the fate of their eternal souls, the pope was ready to let bygones be bygones and granted the crusaders absolution for their crimes. But it wouldn't be long before they would need to seek penance again. While they were still in Zara, an envoy arrived with representatives of a Byzantine named Alexius Angelus. He claimed to be the rightful heir to the Byzantine throne.

According to Alexius, his father Isaac II had been blinded and imprisoned by his uncle, and he, the crown prince, was forced into exile. He was requesting the crusaders' help in reinstating him to the throne. He claimed that once he was restored he would give them 200,000 silver marks, an additional 10,000 men to join their ranks, and would even convert the Greek Orthodox faith of the Byzantines to Catholicism. The idea that this supposed emperor in exile would even be able to do all this should have immediately raised some eyebrows of concern.

But the crusaders' finances were so strained that in the end they couldn't resist. With the Byzantine claimant in tow, the crusaders parked their ships in the Bosporus Strait on July 5th, and unloaded on Constantinople's neighboring suburb of Galata. The crusaders were able to take this city easily, and secure its port. They then moved their attack to the city, where a section of one of the massive city walls of Constantinople was eventually breached. The fighting force was soon repulsed by the Byzantines' numerically superior army, but not before they set fire to a large section of the city.

And as a result, although the crusaders had been defeated, the Byzantine population was so outraged by the damage that they were ready to launch their own internal coup against the usurper to the throne. Feeling the pressure, the imposter fled, and the next day an official envoy was sent to by the Byzantines to the crusader camp informing them that they had restored young Alexius Angelus's father, Isaac II, back to the throne. The crusaders took this as welcome news, even though the original aim was to put their claimant, Alexius, on the throne.

With his father restored, the payment for their services would be deferred to him as leader of the Byzantines. They sent their own envoy back to the Byzantine court and asked Isaac II to fulfill the promises that his son had made to them. Isaac knew that fulfilling such pledges would be impossible, but felt he had no choice but to acquiesce. After receiving his pledge to accept their demands, the crusaders then brought Alexius Angelus into the city, where he was placed in power as a co-emperor next to his blinded father.

As for his debt, Alexius paid half of what he had promised, but couldn't raise enough money for the rest. Several more instances of guile and political intrigue would follow from the Byzantine camp until the crusaders finally had enough and decided to take what they couldn't get through diplomacy, by means of war. The crusaders sacked Constantinople, the city that they had previously pledged to protect.

The pope, of course, was not too happy when he heard about all this, but being several miles away in the Vatican, it was impossible for him to intervene. In the end, the Fourth Crusade was a sad and twisted affair for all those involved. More concerned with financial gain, than anything else, these crusaders never even set foot in the Holy Land. All they really managed to do was weaken the greatest bulwark of Christianity in the Middle East, and pave the way for a complete Islamic takeover in the very near future.

The Last Days of the Crusades

After the Fourth Crusade, the crusades that would follow would make little headway towards that long-stated goal of reclaiming the Holy Land. The next crusade was so meager in its accomplishments that it can be described in less than a paragraph. The fifth official Crusade would only result in the capture of the Egyptian port city of Damietta in 1219, before the crusaders lost the city in 1221, and had to sue for peace with the Egyptian sultan. An eight-year peace agreement was then agreed to, and like clockwork, once eight years had passed, the Sixth Crusade was launched.

This crusade was led by the German Holy Roman Emperor, Frederick II. Amazingly, even less fighting occurred during the Sixth Crusade than in the Fifth. Before a siege of Jerusalem could be ordered, Frederick entered into a peace agreement with the controlling authority of the sultan of Egypt—a figure the crusaders were growing quite familiar with—and managed to regain the Kingdom of Jerusalem under the terms for a ten-year period. When Frederick's followers were informed that the sultan had just handed back the old crusader states without a fight they were overjoyed, but when they heard the stipulations of the agreement they were horrified.

It simply boggled their minds as to why they would be given back the Kingdom of Jerusalem in a lease agreement, renting it out from the sultan for a temporary period. Not only that, but according to the agreement, Jerusalem's walls had to be destroyed, so as to prevent its defense. This would allow Muslim armies to come and take the undefended city back without any difficulty. It was strange for the valiant fighters of the crusades to agree to live under such conditions, to say the least.

And realizing that they were only being tolerated in Jerusalem under the terms of a limited peace agreement, rather than being made the masters of the land, most were completely disgusted.

The Muslim population of Jerusalem were not too happy either, and equally mystified as to why the sultan would agree to such a bizarre treaty. What was the point of allowing Christians to stick around in their backyard for ten years?

For anyone who read the fine print, it really didn't make much sense—except perhaps to Frederick himself—who was ready to take full credit for the agreement and declare it a major win for Christendom. But the truce would begin to break down in just a few years, and Jerusalem would ultimately be invaded by an angry Islamic militia hellbent on driving the Christians out in 1244. This is what led to the Seventh Crusade. The champion of this crusade wouldn't be a German emperor, but rather a French king from the famous "Louis" line.

IX gained an interest in the crusades through his father, Louis VIII (who himself had experience with the enterprise) and when he heard of the disastrous situation in Jerusalem in 1244, he was one of the first European heads of state to take up the cause. King Louis and his men set sail on August 25th, 1248, and on September 17th they docked at a port on the Mediterranean island of Cyprus. From here, Louis led his crusaders back to the old familiar stomping grounds of Damietta, but they were in for a surprise.

When they reached the fortified Egyptian city, it was completely deserted. The defenders, remembering the massacre that the crusaders had wrought just decades before, lost their nerve and retreated to the sultan's camp. Every other man, woman, and child appeared to have followed suit, leading a massive exodus right out on down the Nile. After bolstering his forces, Louis eventually had his men give chase. Progress was slow, however, due to the flooding of the Nile river, and the crusaders had to put up an immense struggle against the elements just to reach Cairo.

They then made their way to the heavily fortified citadel of Al Mansurah, and began their assault. At first things went well for the crusaders, but getting caught up in street-to-street fighting soon proved highly ineffective for the cumbersome knights, and the tide of battle began to change. After suffering heavy losses, including the death of King Louis's own brother Robert, the group decided that they would make a hasty withdrawal back to their holdings in Damietta.

However, they wouldn't make it back to this refuge and would soon be overcome by their Egyptian pursuers, who were much more experienced in traversing the treacherous terrain. Literally stuck in the mud of the Nile, Louis had no choice but to surrender.

It is not entirely clear why, but upon Louis's defeat, the first thing their Muslim captors did was to summarily execute the sick and injured among the crusader ranks. This may have been out of a desire to get rid of those who would be burdensome to escort, or it may have simply been vengeance on the part of the Egyptians.

After this bloodletting, they then took the rest of the crusaders, including Louis himself, hostage. The Egyptian sultan demanded immediate withdrawal from Damietta, and the complete removal of all crusader forces out of Egypt. The government of King Louis also had to pay out a large sum of money in order to secure his release. But right in the midst of King Louis's misery, events would take another sudden turn, when a spontaneous uprising occurred in Egypt and the sultan was overthrown, effectively rendering his previous demands null and void.

The successor quickly realized that they needed the same things for Egypt that the previous sultan had asked, and restated his demands. And so, after all troops were evacuated out of Damietta and at least half of Louis IX's ransom was paid, the

French king returned to Europe empty-handed. He hadn't quite given up though, and continued to follow the affairs of the Middle East over the following decades.

Even when King Louis IX returned to France to govern his kingdom, it is said that thoughts of the Middle East were never very far from his mind. And in the year 1255, it was the tidings of a whole new cast of eastern characters, the Mongols from Central Asia, who captured his full attention once again. Pouring out of the Mongolian steppes like an unstoppable wave, the Mongol warriors caught the entire Muslim world by surprise, smashing right into Persia and Iraq, leaving them completely annihilated in their wake.

The Hidden Christian Kingdom

There had been a legend (or conspiracy theory, if you will) among the crusaders that there was a hidden Christian kingdom in the Far East. This kingdom was said to be ruled by a powerful Christian leader by the name of Prester John, and it had been speculated for years that if only the crusaders could contact this faraway ruler, they would have a natural ally against their Muslim adversaries. With the news of these mysterious new fighters showing up on the eastern borders of the Muslim empire to wreak havoc, many wondered if it was indeed the legendary army of Prester John at work. Since the 1150s, crusaders in Jerusalem had been whispering about the enigmatic figure, sometimes placing him in the Far East, but at other times placing him in Ethiopia, also very far away.

It was the Templars especially who came to believe that Prester John's kingdom was in Ethiopia. Ethiopia was indeed a good candidate for a hidden Christian kingdom. The country's conversion was partially documented in the New Testament itself, in the famous story of Philip and the Ethiopian Eunuch, and was one of the first major nations to become Christian. Though Ethiopia is still predominantly of the same Orthodox Christian faith to this very day, ever since the first wave of Islam knocked out all of the Christian kingdoms in North Africa, Ethiopia became isolated and was for quite a long time the sole Christian nation on the African continent.

So, in many ways, this island of Christianity in East Africa, hidden from potential Christian allies, would indeed appear to fit the profile of the mysterious Kingdom of Prester John. The Templars would later become a bit obsessed with this theory and even came to believe that it was the Ethiopians who had the lost Ark of the Covenant—the mysterious relic of ancient Israel said to hold untold supernatural power. Ethiopia, of course, like this theory too, since it is the Ethiopian Queen of Sheba who famously appeared in the Old Testament as a consort of Israel's King Solomon and—as the Ethiopians have long contended—was possibly the mother of one of Solomon's sons.

The Templars had searched every inch of the ruins of Solomon's Temple in Jerusalem for clues, and they seemed to have come to the conclusion that it was Solomon's son in Ethiopia to which the Ark had been quietly delivered for safekeeping. This is actually a view that Ethiopians themselves have shared for centuries. In the ancient city of Axum in Northern Ethiopia, there is a monastery which to this very day claims to be holding the Ark. None of this has ever been proven, of course, but it was certainly of great interest to many crusaders, the Knights Templar in particular.

But when King Louis and other European leaders heard news of their Muslim enemies being waylaid by mysterious armies coming from the Far East, it wasn't Ethiopia, or any other Christian Kingdom at work, it was the Mongol horde that was created by Genghis Khan. And as Louis and all other potential crusaders would soon find out, the khan's army would kill Christians just as easily as they would Muslims. When it came to world domination, these bloodthirsty conquerors did not discriminate.

From Prester John to Genghis Khan

The Christian world initially believed their prayers had been answered when they received word that a new army had risen up in the East to take down their Muslim adversaries, but if they were hoping for an ally to their own crusades in the Holy Land, they would be sorely disappointed. Both the pope and King Louis had entered into official correspondence with the Khan leadership, and both were mocked and rejected for their overtures outright.

They now knew exactly who they were dealing with, and as the Mongol horde was pushing closer toward the crusader states in the Holy Land, the European powers knew that after the Muslim nations were steamrolled, the Holy Land would be next. But fate had something else in store. Just when the Mongols were at the crusaders' doorstep, their leader back home, the "Great Khan," died. These tidings put the overstretched Mongol forces in disarray, and the last Muslim stronghold not to be severely challenged by the Mongols—Egypt—rose up to repel the Mongol horde.

The Christians would actually have Egyptian Muslims to thank for sparing them from complete destruction at the hands of the Mongols. But it would be the Egyptians themselves who would soon prove to be the next threat the crusader kingdom would face. Egyptian forces had conducted a massive raid on Galilee in 1263, and completely laid waste to the cathedral of Nazareth. Then, in 1268, they conquered the port of Jaffa, terrorizing its residents into submission.

Jaffa was then used as a springboard to attack Antioch, which quickly fell to the determined force of Egypt's resurgent sultan. The assault on Antioch was a complete massacre. As soon as the sultan's men were inside the city they shut the gates behind them, trapping the residents inside. Men, women, and children were all put to the sword. Antioch had been in crusader hands for 170 years, and now the streets ran red with Christian blood.

This is what moved the French King Louis to lead the charge for an Eighth Crusade. This crusade disembarked in the summer of 1270. The immediate destination of these crusaders wasn't the Holy Land, and it wasn't Egypt either. It was actually the North African nation of Tunis that would be the staging ground for this conflict. Tunisia, of course, would someday be a French colony, and some have tried to theorize that this crusade itself was an early attempt at colonization. But by all accounts, Tunis was to be a staging ground for the invasion of Egypt, and there were no plans for a permanent stay in the region.

Louis and his fellow crusaders landed in Tunisia on July 18th. They made camp in the ruins of the ancient city of Carthage; here Louis waited for more reinforcements to arrive before beginning the main course of the operation.

As they waited for additional troops to arrive they were subjected to periodic raids by Muslim militias. But these were of minor consequence when compared to the true danger the waiting crusaders faced—lethal outbreaks of disease in their camp. Malaria and other ailments began to afflict the army, and a large chunk of the fighting force either died from the pestilence or were incapacitated by it.

Even the king wasn't immune to these invisible killers, and soon he, too, succumbed to the illness. On August 25th, having coming down with a tremendous fever (in which he was heard to deliriously shout, "Jerusalem! Jerusalem!") King Louis IX died, closing the chapter on the Eighth Crusade with his passing.

The sun would soon set on the whole crusader kingdom as well. The armies of Islam laid siege to last great stronghold of Christendom in the Holy Land, the fortified city of Acre, on April 6th, 1291.

The crusaders were greatly outnumbered and on May 18th, their relentless opponents managed to tear down part of Acre's mighty walls, and they poured into the city. Knowing that disaster was imminent, the crusaders evacuated women and children onto boats docked in the harbor as the Christian knights continued their desperate fight. The highly disciplined military orders of the Templars, Hospitallers, and Teutonic Knights in particular fought with bold ferocity, as the conflict turned into intense street fighting inside Acre.

But nevertheless, the Muslim onslaught was too great to turn back, and by nightfall the remaining crusaders had all been pushed back toward the harbor, where they holed up inside the "Templar's House." In this former base for the monastic order, the last remaining knights of the crusade made their last stand. At one point during the standoff the cornered fighters agreed to surrender for the sake of evacuating some of the remaining civilians who had sought refuge with them. It was then agreed that everyone with the knights would have safe passage upon surrender.

But when Muslim fighters entered the compound they began to manhandle and attempt to forcibly remove several of the women and young men, apparently with the intention of selling them on the slave market. Seeing this brutality rekindled the fiery rage of the crusaders and they intervened, rescuing the would-be hostages, and driving the Muslims out of the building. Their assailants were amazed, and marveled at the tenacity of these few warriors who were still mounting such an effective defense.

The leaders of the siege did not want to waste any more time attacking a trapped opponent, however; and so instead they decided to just blow the wall right off the building by planting mines near the foundation. But they misjudged their handiwork, and accidentally caused the entire building to collapse, killing everyone inside. And with the Templar House, so too collapsed Christian Europe's dreams of a Christian presence in the Holy Land.

The Final Crusaders and The Dangers Within

After the fall of the mainland crusader states, the only possession left to the Christians from the crusader era was the island of Cyprus. It was here that the Knights Templar set up their base. The Templars were the monastic order that seemed to receive the most blame and criticism for the fall of Jerusalem, and now that their days of protecting the Holy Land seemed all but over. They were often looked at with scorn and their wealthy houses, temples, and lodges in Cyprus (and all across Europe) were the subject of speculation and open suspicion.

The Templars were indeed rich. Their wealth came from a combination of steady donations from supporters as well as lands they owned and treasures they had collected during their time in the Holy Land. King Philip IV of France in particular began to plot against the Templars, in order to put down potential rivals, but more importantly, to obtain their wealth for himself. This led him to concoct a scheme to arrest all the Templars in France on charges of heresy.

He made good on this plan on Friday, October 13th, 1307. The Templars were taken completely unaware on that very bad Friday the 13th, which is why we still refer to the day as an unlucky one. These members of the Knights Templar were then subjected to horrible abuse and torture, until they confessed—to fabricated charges. The crusaders were forced to admit to everything from black magic and heresy to engaging in sodomy. The leader of the Knights Templar (the grand master) was then burned at the stake in public.

Historians generally agree that King Philip trumped up these charges because he wished to get his hands on the wealth and power of the Knights Templar for himself, and the pope agreed because he wished to curry the favor of the powerful French king. But there is a conspiracy theory that makes this story just a little bit more complicated than that. There are those who say that it wasn't the Templars' money, power, or prestige that the Church was after, but rather, their *secrets.*

Proponents of this conspiracy theory claim that the Catholic Church found out that the Templars had stumbled upon a heretical secret during their time in the Holy Land, and wanted to suppress it. These theorists contend that during their time in Jerusalem, the Knights had found some documentation proving that Jesus had a wife named Mary Magdalene, and the fabled Holy Grail was actually her womb, which had carried Jesus's child. According to this theory, Mary was then spirited off to southern France, where she gave birth to the first in a long line of kings known as the Merovingians.

It was supposedly the threat of this information leaking out to the general public that the Church and the government of France sought to avoid by besmirching the character of the Knights Templar with false accusations, and then permanently silencing them by burning them at the stake. For many others, however, such claims are completely unfounded and more than a bit outrageous. But whatever the case may be, the Templars were virtually exterminated.

Although it has not been proven, it is theorized that a few survivors of the Knights Templar managed to escape to Scotland, and that the modern-day Freemasons originate from this final remnant of the Knights Templar. This theory is rejected by modern Freemasons however, who point out that freemasonry has apparent influences from all of the monastic orders, not just the Knights Templar.

After the destruction of the Templars in the early fourteenth century, the Hospitaller Knights became the largest monastic order, and soon they began to worry that they would be the next to be targeted. Hoping to avoid the same fate, they sought to prove themselves useful and began to engage in military operations that they thought would cast them in a good light with the pope and other European powers. This idea was a primary motivator when the Hospitallers launched an attack on the Greek island of Rhodes in 1307. These former crusaders then went about turning the island into a strategic fortress, to serve as a kind of watchtower on the East.

Another watchtower was the remnant of the Kingdom of Jerusalem that had moved to the neighboring island of Cyprus. Working like a government in exile, the residents of Cyprus were also anxiously awaiting the next crusade. Their king, Peter I, who claimed direct succession from the former Kings of Jerusalem, eventually left the island to embark upon a grand tour all across Europe, during which he spoke to several heads of state in an effort to galvanize another crusade.

To the surprise of many, he did manage to summon a rather modest force, and brought it to Rhodes in 1365 in order to prepare an invasion of the Holy Land. They then launched from their base of operations and traveled by sea to the famous port of Alexandria, Egypt, on October 9th. The citizens of Alexandria were apparently unaware of what was happening, and took the strangers to be merchant vessels from Europe.

Not expecting any danger, they allowed them to set anchor unimpeded, and waltz right through the gate. They would come to regret it. The crusaders ran loose through the city and cut down anyone who stood in their way. They took the city by force in just one day.

But soon after Alexandria's capture, Peter was shocked to find his men speaking of their desire to drop everything and go home. Apparently, after getting their fill of loot and other spoils of war, they simply wished to return to Europe with their riches. Peter stressed to the men the importance of keeping and holding this major North

African port city, but none of them were interested. After a so-called "council of war" was convened, the leading members of the contingency agreed that they would rather quit while they were ahead, instead of struggling to defend this Egyptian metropolis. Peter couldn't believe what he was hearing.

He knew that the creation of a permanent base in Alexandria would be the best opportunity that the crusaders had had in several decades for the retaking of the Holy Land. It would have been the perfect launchpad for repeated attempts to reclaim lost territory. But this king-in-exile seemed to be the only one who thought this way. And when the sultan of Egypt moved toward the city, everyone else quickly disbanded and left. It is said that Peter himself was the very last to leave, pleading with his brethren to reconsider until the very last minute of their evacuation.

When word got back to the European heads of state that such an opportunity had been squandered, they were just as disgusted as Peter, and sympathized deeply with his plight. But even so, they were not ready to lend out any more aid in the form of men or money for any future endeavors. Peter eventually went back to Cyprus a broken man. After his great expenditure in Alexandria he was broken both spiritually and financially, and his peers in Cyprus were none too happy about it.

As the animosity of his own countrymen began to build around him, sadly, he was assassinated. It is said he was murdered in his own bedchamber. He had traveled hundreds of miles to face down Christendom's biggest foe and came home only to be killed in his own bed. Little did his killers know, they were most likely signing the death warrant for Cyprus by doing so.

And after years of decline thereafter, Cyprus was taken into Muslim dominion, as a newly united Islamic empire continued to expand in scope and power. All in all, the 1300s were a rather unlucky time period for the Crusades and Christendom, and both remained in constant danger from within as well as without.

The Ottoman Empire and the Canceled Crusade

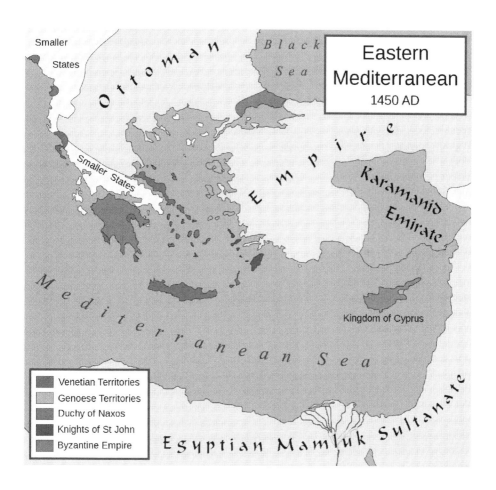

The Islamic polity that became known as the Ottoman Empire first came to prominence in Asia Minor (modern-day Turkey) in the fourteenth century, as various Turkish tribes began to unite.

The founder of this unification was the Turkish leader Osman, who led rapid territorial acquisitions of formerly Greek Byzantine lands and the neighboring Balkans. This trend steadily continued even after Osman's death, and by the early fifteenth century, the Byzantine Empire was little more than a city-state.

Practically every inch of land outside Constantinople's walls had been absorbed into the Empire of the Ottoman Turks. After working their way right up to its gates, in 1422 the Ottoman Empire began laying siege to Constantinople itself. Ottoman Sultan Murad II led a massive assault on Constantinople on June 8th, 1422. The Byzantines, whose population had been in rapid decline for centuries, were entirely outnumbered, and most likely would have perished rather quickly in a head-on engagement.

Fortunately for them, however, they wouldn't have to face that challenge; their fortifications held out. The Turks, simply unable to break through their defenses, had to call off the attack. The Byzantines were lucky to have survived, but the emperor knew that neither their fortune nor their walls would last forever. He knew he had to call on the West for help—he knew he had to ask for another crusade. But he also knew that it would take much more convincing now than it had in the past to bring about such a result.

And the Byzantines, threadbare now, didn't have much to offer, but the crafty emperor knew he still had one thing that the pope wanted more than anything else—an official conversion of his realm to Catholicism. He knew that if he could convince the pope that his people would trade in their Orthodox faith to unite with the West under the Catholic banner, the pope would do everything in his power to send the best crusading force Europe could muster.

It was in this last-ditch effort for aid that Byzantine Emperor, John II, and the patriarch of Constantinople personally attended the Council of Florence in 1437. Here the emperor and the patriarch engaged the pope and other clergy in open, honest debate, discussing the finer points of theology for hours on end. Finally, after ironing out their differences and finding some common ground that they could rally behind, Emperor John II placed his signature on an agreement that signaled that the eastern churches would be reunited with the Catholic Church of the West.

It was on January 1st, 1443, that the pope excitedly sent off the alarm all throughout Europe and called for a brand new crusade to help salvage what was left of the Byzantine Empire. The usual players of Germany, France, and England were non-responsive, due to too much internal strife. Instead, the main respondents to the call were Poland, Wallachia, and Hungary. These countries clearly understood the threat, because they were already on the front lines due to the encroachments of the Turks right in their own backyard, the Balkans.

In the first engagement of this crusade, these Eastern European powers sent a force of about 20,000 soldiers into Serbia in 1444, and managed to capture the Serbian town of Nish, which had been recently overrun by the Turks. The crusaders then marched on to the city of Varna. Here they would meet a bad end, when a large contingent of fresh troops sent from the Ottoman Empire intercepted the crusaders and defeated them utterly.

Another crusade ended without even reaching its intended target. The Byzantines, meanwhile, were being pressed more and more with every passing day. Ottoman Sultan Mehmed II began to set into motion what would be the final campaign against the Byzantines, by positioning his army across the Bosporus, and effectively closing off the great city of

Constantinople. This was meant to keep any further outside help from arriving, but even with their troops strangling off access to the city in this manner, it is said that several hundred Italian crusaders managed to slip by to join the Byzantines in their struggle.

The Byzantines did everything they could to bolster their defenses. They reinforced every wall, barrier, and trench they could find. And to prevent access from the sea, they even chained up Constantinople's docks so enemy vessels wouldn't be able park in them. But as always, the main defense of the Byzantines would be their thick city walls.

The Ottomans had a surprise for the Byzantines, however, and upon advancing to the gates of the city in April of 1453, they placed a large cannon on the battlefield. They then aimed it at a section of the Byzantine wall and began firing. They hoped that their new weapon would be able to make short work of the defensive structure, but they would be disappointed. After several direct hits, the walls were barely even damaged. This led some of the Turks to whisper to themselves that the walls must be made of solid steel in order to withstand the blast. At any rate, Mehmed grew impatient with the results, and decided to change tactics. Giving up on the cannon for the time being, he sent out some of his engineers to see if they could tunnel underneath the barrier, but this proved futile as well.

The Ottomans had no choice but to simply use the bulk of their army and brute force to push their way in, and in late May of 1453 the Sultan's troops charged into the city. A massacre bordering on genocide followed as the common citizens of Constantinople bore the brunt of centuries of the Turks' stored-up hatred and animosity toward the Byzantine Empire.

The fall of Constantinople had been imminent for a while, and yet it still came as a shock to the western world. Even though it had been tottering near collapse for quite some time, the Byzantines had been in place for so long, it was hard for most to imagine that they would really fall. And now that the Christian bulwark of the Byzantines was no longer in place to check the Muslim advance, the Turkish military machine was free to march right into the heart of Europe. The pope's reaction was fairly predictable, one of mourning and great dismay, before calling upon Europe for another crusade.

But Europe, still embroiled in its own petty rivalries, was just not ready for the commitment. Meanwhile, the survivors of the Byzantine Empire's collapse began to flood into Western Europe, bringing with them new knowledge and skills that would forever change the face of western society, leading to new discoveries, and in 1492, even a whole new continent. The Byzantine Empire and the ambition of Europe's crusaders were annihilated, but flowers would yet bloom from the ashes.

After the fall of Constantinople, for the western world, Islam seemed destined to rise just as much as Christianity seemed destined to fall. Christianity was being surrounded on all sides and there seemed to be no escape in sight. And as the noose tightened around European Christendom even the old trade routes on which Europe depended were inaccessible. With the Ottoman capture of Constantinople, all access to the East by land was essentially blocked off.

This then led to the vigorous search for new trade routes to the Orient. And in 1492, a man named Christopher Columbus was given the task of finding a new sea route to the East. For many of us today this seems like a lot of work just to be able to bring back spices from Asia, but there are those who theorize that Columbus and his collaborators had much more than salt and pepper on their minds. Because according to some theorists, much more than the establishment of a new trade route, Columbus was actually looking for a new crusade.

Columbus was a deeply religious man, and it is well documented in many of his final writings that he longed to raise money and contribute to the creation of another crusade. He believed that it was his destiny to help orchestrate a return to the Holy Land, and he held many apocalyptic ideas regarding that event. He seemed to believe that a Christian return to the Holy Land would begin some sort of countdown to the fulfillment of biblical prophecy.

Columbus also claimed to have personally seen visions, and once announced his firm belief that the world would end in 1650. But regardless of some of his stranger beliefs, Columbus was a true visionary. And although he didn't find a new trade route to Asia, or kick start a new crusade, he did discover America, and change the course of European history as a result.

Without the massive influx of wealth that the discovery of the Americas would soon bring to the western world, the armies of Islam may well have completely subdued it. As Europe was being pressured with invasion from the east, new discoveries further west would give European Christendom the release valve it needed to survive. Since the time of the First Crusade there have been actions and reactions that have led the world to where it is today.

The Lesser Crusades and the Sick Man of Europe

In the year 1499, Christian Europe received another blow from the rapidly expanding Ottoman Empire. It was that year that the Republic of Venice lost control of the city of Lepanto as it was overrun by the Ottomans. It was less than fifty years since the fall of Constantinople, and although the Europeans held a major trump card with the discovery of America in 1492, it would be several more decades before they fully understood what it was they had discovered, and how to turn it to their advantage.

In the meantime, the armies of Islam were on the move and threatening to snuff out western civilization once and for all. Some may feel that such words are an exaggeration, but they are based on fact. The Ottoman Turks of this time period were firm believers in the precepts of "Dar al-Islam" (House of Islam) and "Dar al-Harb" (House of War). For those who followed this teaching, any civilization living outside of "Dar al-Islam" (the House of Islam) was by default in a "House of War," needing to be brought under the submission of Islam by force. This was how world peace was to be brought about.

In this teaching, peace can only be brought about by forced conquest at the hands of Islam, and this was the goal of the Ottoman Empire of this time period. In 1499, they seemed perfectly poised to fulfill their commission of world domination. Ottoman Admiral Kemal Reis had taken command of the Ottoman fleet in the Mediterranean, and sent it smashing into the Venetian navy. The Ottomans were able to overpower the Venetians and broke through their lines to capture the small, but strategic, island of Lepanto.

This was of grave concern for the Venetians because the island was a good stepping stone for an all-out invasion of the Republic of Venice. This imminent danger continued to hang over the heads of Europe for several years. And with the threat of militant Islam right at his doorstep, the pope in neighboring Rome decided to call for yet another crusade. The terminology was different at this point, and the pope would actually refer to the group of Christian fighters he cobbled together as a "Holy League" but this group of defenders were in every sense a new generation of crusaders in all but name.

Made up of participants from Genoa, Spain, Malta, Parma, Tuscany, and the Papal State itself, this Holy League knew that they were the last thing blocking an outright invasion of Western Europe. These Holy League crusaders amassed their forces and launched a naval fleet made up of six big Venetian ships called *galleasses*, as well as 207 smaller galleys, which carried a total of 30,000 men. This armada reached Lepanto in October of 1571, and on October 7th, the battle began in earnest. The Venetian cruisers were said to be the best equipped in the engagement, but what the Turks did not have in equipment they more than made up with sheer manpower.

The Ottoman fleet was said to have been manned by over 100,000 men, with ships spanning nearly the entire breadth of the Mediterranean. This was certainly an intimidating sight, but the crusaders continued forward. Their secret weapons were the six Venetian Galleass ships. These had just recently been developed by the Republic of Venice by converting large merchant ships into military freighters. These ships were bigger and slower than other seafaring vessels but they were sturdy— and more importantly, they were bristling with the most advanced and deadly cannon technology from top to bottom.

The Ottomans had never heard of these innovative ships before, and seeing what they believed to be just helpless merchant vessels break rank they immediately sent several ships in pursuit. They were under the false impression that the Venetians had made a mistake and left their merchant ships vulnerable, and they didn't hesitate to take advantage of this, thinking there would be valuables to plunder from the vessels. This would prove to be a deadly mistake.

As soon as the Turkish ships drew near, the powerful guns of the Venetian galleasses let loose on them, obliterating 70 Turkish ships without much of a fight in return. The crusaders then received another bit of good luck when the headwinds blew in their favor, allowing them to head at full speed right into the Ottoman ships. The crusader ships were then able to mercilessly pummel these vessels as they became like sitting ducks, stuck in place.

The Ottoman galley *Sultana* sought to intervene in this free-for-all, and using the hundreds of slaves chained at its oars, propelled itself right into the side of one of the leading crusader ships. Turkish fighters then poured out of the *Sultana* and engaged the Christian crusaders in a pitched battle spanning the decks of both ships. Shortly thereafter, the Ottoman's captain, Ali Pasha, was killed and the crusaders of the Holy League were able to board the vessel and take it over.

The Ottoman fleet was then forced to surrender in one of the biggest defeats the Ottoman Empire would ever face. The crusaders not only gained possession of the Ottoman navy, but also their cargo—which included 15,000 Christian slaves that they were able to free from bondage. These were men and women who had either been captured by Ottoman pirates on the high seas, or who were prisoners of war enslaved by the Turks and made to row in their galleys.

As these slaves were freed from bondage, all of Europe breathed a sigh of relief that its own yoke of bondage in the Mediterranean had been broken. But despite their victory on the sea, the Ottomans were still rapidly advancing on land, and their next major assault on Europe would take them all the way to Vienna, Austria in September of 1683. This epic battle was aptly called the "Battle of Vienna" and involved a 90,000-strong Ottoman invasion force.

Upon the Sultan's arrival in Vienna, one of his messengers famously delivered a message on his behalf, advising his adversaries, "Accept Islam and live in peace under the Sultan." Adhering to the precepts of Dar-al-Islam, the Ottomans clearly believed there could only be peace in the world when everyone submitted to their leader and his personal take on religion. But after this ultimatum was given the citizens of Vienna promptly turned down the Sultan's idea of "peace" through submission, and prepared to defend themselves.

After they rejected his proposal, the Sultan laid siege to the city. Vienna was completely encircled, but the Viennese held on and mounted a formidable defense. Realizing that taking the city in an all-out assault would be costly, the Ottomans decided to change tactics and began digging under the walls and planting mines instead. In this manner they hoped to cause a section of the wall to collapse so that they could simply pour inside after the smoke had cleared.

The city's defenders were ready, however, and were able to dig their own counter tunnels, mine them, and then blow them up, causing the Ottomans tunnels to collapse, killing several Ottomans in the process. But the walls were taking a serious beating in the process and the defenders of the city had, at this point, already been reduced to a force of not much more than 4000. Things were bleak for Vienna, and despite their best efforts, they could literally see the writing on the wall—soon they would indeed be forced to submit to the "peace" that the Ottoman Empire wished to bestow upon them.

But then something happened. Right at the last minute, when Vienna was on the verge of complete and total collapse, the glint of armor could be seen in the distance. An army of over 60,000 men appeared, marching across the western horizon. Holy League or Crusade, (whatever you want to call it), the pope, knowing what Vienna was facing, had managed to cobble together various factions of Europe led by King John III of Poland, and send them to the rescue. Call it a Holy League, or call it a Crusade, all the besieged citizens of Vienna knew was that the cavalry had arrived.

The Crusader army had marched over mountains and through forests and other treacherous terrain just to get to the battlefield, and if they had arrived even an hour later, Vienna most likely would already have been crushed. But providence, fate, fortune, whatever you want to call it, seemed to come together to allow these crusaders to come to the city's aid in its most desperate hour. The Ottomans, knowing just how difficult such a crossing would be, never dreamed that it would be attempted, and as a result left their western flank completely open to attack.

So, on that September 11th morning of 1683, when the Holy League burst through the woods to confront them, they didn't have a chance. The Ottoman general, Kara Mustafa, was unable to coordinate his troops in time. The Crusaders charged and tore right through their ranks. In fairly short order, the Ottomans were forced into a hasty retreat, back to their frontier base in the Balkans. This was a major turning point in the centuries-long conflict often referred to as the wars of the "Cross and the Crescent."

The Ottoman juggernaut had hitherto appeared unstoppable and was about to claw right through the heart of Western Europe, but it was indeed stopped on that September 11th. After the Ottomans failed to take Austria, the Ottoman Empire entered into a long, slow decline. And losing much of its prestige and power as it withered away, it would become known as the sick man of Europe. That sick man of the Ottoman Empire ultimately died on November 1st, 1922, leaving the country of Turkey as its only successor state.

After this collapse, most in the twentieth century believed the threat of radical Islam to be long behind them. It wouldn't be until the beginning of the 21st Century, on yet another infamous September 11th in 2001, that most would became aware of this existential threat once again. The crusades happened a long time ago, yet they remain relevant, returning to our conversations to this very day. Is this a conspiracy? Or just the sound of history repeating itself?

The Conspiracy of Silence

In recent years so much has been said and written about the Crusades it can be rather difficult to sort through it all. Yet at the same time, the Crusades are still one of the most misunderstood events in all history.

No one doubts the bravery of the soldiers of Normandy who pushed back the Nazi advance during World War II, but when it comes to the men who gave their lives to protect all of Europe on September 11th, 1683, at the gates of Vienna—the silence is deafening. Because, truth be told, when it comes to the Crusades, the greatest conspiracy is the conspiracy of silence.

Christianity in the middle ages was more vulnerable than is comfortable to consider, and without the crusaders, western civilization as we know it today might not even exist. What we should keep in mind is how different the world would look today, if not for the initiative and bravery of the men who stood against the spread of Islam.

Also by Conrad Bauer

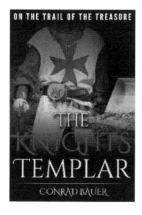 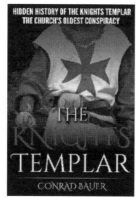 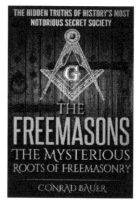

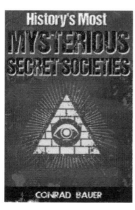  

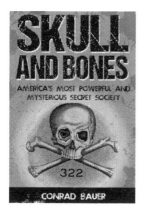  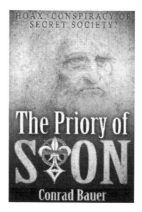

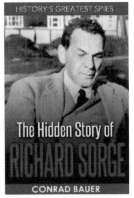

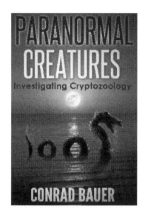

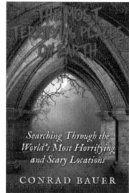

Appendix A: Further Reading and References

As we draw this book to a close I would like to share with you the reading materials and references that helped to make this book possible. If you are interested in any of the topics broached and discussed in this book, I highly recommend looking into these valuable resources.

The Crusades: A Short History, Jonathan Riley-Smith
Jonathan Riley-Smith has long been an expert on the Crusades and this book does not disappoint. Covering just about every Crusade and pseudo-Crusade ever launched, if you need in-depth material about the Crusades this book will give it to you.

The New Concise History of the Crusades, Thomas F. Madden
Madden's book on the Crusades not only provides an excellent historic timeline, but also in-depth stories about personal motivations on all sides of the Crusades. As contentious as the Crusades are, Madden manages to remain neutral and non-biased in tone, and just present the facts at face value. If you would like a clear and balanced view of what really happened during the time of the Crusades, this book is highly recommended.

The Crusades Through Arab Eyes, Amin Maalouf
Many today who have heard quite a bit of European accounts of the Crusades are hungry for information from the other side of the conflict and Amin's book, *The Crusades Through Arab Eyes* does just that. Until he wrote this book, alternate views on the Crusades were rather scarce, but Mr. Maalouf really did his work and pieced together every account, every testament and lost

chronicle, to provide the missing puzzle pieces we need to fully understand the Crusades.

The Secret History of Freemasonry, Paul Naudon
This book provides a rare insight into the world of the Freemasons and the origins that trace it back to the Crusades. If you are looking for an in-depth repository of historical information about Freemasonry, this book is a great place to start.

The Origin of Freemasonry and Knights Templar, John Bennet
This book not only speaks about Freemasonry but ties it directly back to the Knights Templar, the Crusades, and the very Temple Mount of Jerusalem. This book is eye-opening in its implications and is a highly recommended read.

Conspiracies and Secret Societies, Brad and Sherry Steiger
Brad Steiger is a well-known author of the paranormal and here in this massive volume on the subject of conspiracies, he and his wife Sherry really outdo themselves in the sheer comprehensiveness of this volume. Literally from A to Z, every single conspiracy that has ever been uttered under the sun is in this book. As for the Crusades in particular, the information on the Knights Templar, hidden relics, as well as hidden motives, are all covered here in depth. If you have an interest in conspiracies and the Crusades, you have just got to read this!

Image Credits

Marching Toward Holy Ground -
https://commons.wikimedia.org/wiki/File:Godfrey_of_Bouillon_and_leaders_of_the_first_crusade.gif

Map of Roman Empire in 116 A.D. -
https://commons.wikimedia.org/wiki/File:Roman_Empire_in_116_AD.png

The People's Crusade and Other Misadventures -
https://commons.wikimedia.org/wiki/File:Peter_the_Hermit_Preaching_the_First_Crusade.jpg

The Real Crusade Begins - https://pixabay.com/en/crusader-knight-warrior-battle-2200579/

Holy Land in Crusading Hands -
https://commons.wikimedia.org/wiki/File:Philpot,_Glyn_Warren;_Richard_I_Leaving_England_for_the_Cr
usades,_1189;_Parliamentary_Art_Collection.jpg

The "Kingdom of Heaven" is at Hand - https://commons.wikimedia.org/wiki/File:Israel-2013-Jerusalem-
Temple_Mount-Al-Aqsa_Mosque_(NE_exposure).jpg

The Second Crusade -
https://commons.wikimedia.org/wiki/File%3ASiege_of_Damascus%2C_second_crusade.jpg

The Third Crusade and the Leper King -
https://commons.wikimedia.org/wiki/File:Counquest_of_Jeusalem_(1099).jpg

The Great Miracle -
https://commons.wikimedia.org/wiki/File:Crusaders_before_Jerusalem_MET_ep87.15.110.jpg

The Last Days of the Crusades - https://commons.wikimedia.org/wiki/File:2007templar1--maxweb.jpg

The Hidden Christian Kingdom-
https://commons.wikimedia.org/wiki/File:The_Church_of_Abba_Afse,_Yeha,_Tigray_Region,_Northern_E
thiopia_(3133387451).jpg

The Final Crusaders and The Dangers Within - https://commons.wikimedia.org/wiki/File:Knights-
templar.jpg

The Ottoman Empire and the Canceled Crusade -
https://commons.wikimedia.org/wiki/File:Eastern_Mediterranean_1450.svg

The Lesser Crusades and the Sick Man of Europe - https://sites.google.com/site/worldwar1class4/war-in-
the-middle-east/the-arab-revolt

Made in United States
Orlando, FL
22 June 2023

34429788R00054